A Literary Diva's Guide to Starting a Fab Book Club

How to Create a Book Club in 7 Easy Steps

Joy C. Farrington

A Literary Diva

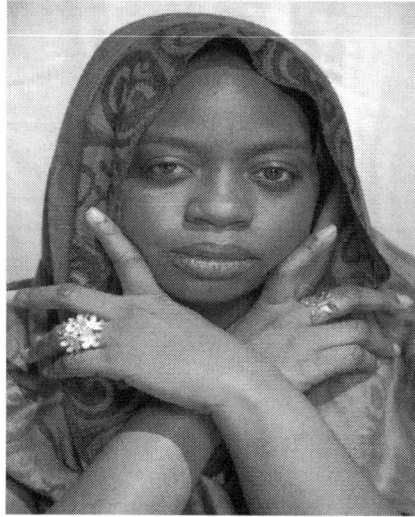

Joy Farrington is CEO of Lit Diva, Inc. a non-profit organization that supports, promotes, and empowers African-American book clubs and authors through event planning, online marketing, and public relations. Lit Diva, Inc. entities includes: Nubian Literary Network, Nubian Lit News and the Lit Diva Network.

Ms. Farrington, also known as the Book Club Expert, is president of Nubian Sistas Book Club. Created in 2004, Nubian Sistas Book Club has been nominated for various awards including the 3rd Annual Marguerite Press Awards for Best Promoter and Best Website and are the proud winners of the 2004 Disilgold Most Aspiring Breakthrough Book Club of the Year and Best New Book Club. She is also the editor of the Review Divas, Book Review Team and has personally been nominated for several literary awards.

She lives in Miami, Florida.

Printed in the USA
Lulu Press

Lit Diva, Inc.
18520 NW 67th Ave
Suite 241
Miami, Fl 33015
nubianlit@gmail.com

Dedication

This book is dedicated to my son, Daelon,
growing stronger and smarter every day.
Mommy loves you.

and

To my brother, Ferron,
resting in peace in the City of Angels.
I miss you.

Acknowledgments

To my son, Daelon for being my motivation, my heart, my everything.

To my family: my sister, Michaelle, my cousins, Crystal, Keisha, Monique, Nicky, Sean, Sainabou, broh-in law, Ralph, my aunts, uncles, grandma and my parents, Jo and Mikey, thank you for always being in my corner and supporting all my crazy idea- well most of them anyways.

To my BFFs, Nicky D., and Mac: "You're not always there when I call, but you're always on time." I LOVE YOU MAN, lol.

To my editor, Pittershawn Palmer, thank your doing such a great job.

To Literary Divas, Moody Holiday, Electa Rome Park, Denise Turney, Joylynn Jossell, Desiree Dalton, Black Coffee, Diane Bromfield, and the Ladies of O.O.S.A , thank you for your contribution and insights without which this book wouldn't be the same.

To Andrew Morrison and all the members of the Book in 30 FaceBook Group, your support and information helped make this dream into a reality.

To my business coach, Monikah Ogando, for never taking my "buts" for an answer.

To all the members, past and present of Nubian Sistas Book Club, thank you for sharing your love of books with me.

Table of Contents

Preface

A Literary Diva's Guide... is a series of books and workshops geared to aid book club members in creating, hosting and maintaining a book club.

The series also caters to self published authors seeking ways to promote their books through online marketing, social media, and book club marketing.

Throughout the series, readers will discover ways to organize a meeting, activities to include in your meeting, over 100 Book of the Month suggestions, resource guides, an agenda template, marketing tips, tools, event planning and more.

It is my hope my books will be used as an integral tool by every book club looking for fun and innovative ways to start or enhance a club as well as new and self published authors hoping to take their book marketing up a notch. For more information regarding this and other titles please visit www.thebookclubexpert.com

Are you a Literary Diva?

Would you like to be?

If so, join the Lit Diva Network at www.imalitdiva.com

 The Lit Diva Network was created for women who are passionate about reading and likes to implement the literary world into their daily lives. LDN members includes: avid readers, book club members, as well as book lovers who took their passion for books into a business.

During your membership with LDN you will receive a variety of guides, books, and giveaways. Each month features a different informative topic, free gifts, and surprises created with the sole purpose of keeping our members engaged and on their toes.

Founded by Joy Farrington, The Book Club Expert, LDN is THE place where book lovers can engage with other readers and stay connected with the Literary World.

Membership Includes:

- *A Lit Diva Guide to Starting a Book Club* Workbook
- *Help! My Book Club is Driving Me Crazy* Idea Guide
- Discounts on All Lit Diva Network Sponsored Events

- Lit Diva e-courses and Teleconferences
- Exclusive access to our Lit Diva Forum
- Quarterly Issues of our *Between the Sheets* Booklet featuring Book of the Month Selections, Reading Guides, Author Interview, Event Calendars and more…

Visit us online at www.imalitdiva.com for more information.

Introduction

So, you want to start a book club. Congratulations, you are taking the first steps in joining the ranks of other literary divas throughout the ages. Although the idea of starting a club may seem daunting at first, you'll be surprised how easy it really is. In this e-book, I created 7 easy steps that will get your club started in no time. By following this simple process I guarantee you will have a club up and running within in no time.

Chapter 1

What's Your Purpose?

Knowing the purpose of your club is important to know in the beginning process of starting a book club. Your purpose is the underlying reason for creating your club.

It can ranged from women empowerment to starting a club to encourage teens to read. Your book club could focus only on African-American (AA) books, be exclusive for females, classic novels or to follow Oprah's Book Club Selection.

When thinking about the type of club you would like to create, ask yourself the following questions:

1. Would you like to open your membership to the public or have membership by invitation only?

2. What kind of books would you like to read? Are you interested in urban, erotica, romance, the classics, sci-fi or horror? Your club can read a variety of genres or concentrate on just one topic.

3. Do you want a club open to all ages, men and women, or females only?

4. Will this club me more social, academic, or an outreach program?

Chapter Two
Book-It

Pick your BOTM before the meeting and give your potential members enough time to read it by providing at least three to four weeks advance notice. Also, select a book of the month that fits into the type of club you plan to create. If you would like a club that reads mostly urban books, picking a book from Oprah's Book Club would not be wise. Pick a book that will engage the reader from the beginning. Also, books that are thought provoking will provide the most engaging book discussion. Selecting a book on a whim is not a good idea, so you're going to have to do some research here.

A great first BOTM is important because one of the hardest parts of maintaining a book club is motivating members to read the book. If your first selection isn't interesting, you may not even get people to come to your first meeting because they never finished the book.

A few book titles my book club enjoyed are: *Them* by Nathan McCall, *Fly on the Wall* by Trista Russell, *The Other Brother* by Brandon Massey, *I Know Why the Caged Bird Sings* by Maya Angelou and *Addicted* by Zane. For a more thorough list of BOTMs compiled by genres and a list of recommended book review sites, read *A Literary Diva's Guide to Hosting a Fab Book Club Meeting*. In the book, I compiled a list of over 100 books from a variety of genres that will last you throughout the year.

Chapter 3
The Place to Be

Your location will set the mood for your first meeting. For example, if you choose to have it in a restaurant, your meeting will have a more social feel.

Consider the type of book club meeting you would like to have when picking a location. If you would like a more social club, go to a restaurant. But if you plan a more scholarly club maybe a book store would better fit your needs. Also, for safety reasons, if your book club is open to the public, have your meeting in a location like a library or book store instead of your home.

Pick a date and time you think would fit everyone's schedule. For example, late Sunday afternoons and 7pm during the week work best for my club, Nubian Sistas. Do a quick survey by sending everyone a message asking them when they will be available. A great survey site is http://polldaddy.com. This gives potential members the option of selecting three or four different times and dates. Use the results from the survey as a way to help pick the best feasible time for the club meeting. However, don't stress yourself by trying to please everyone. There will always be one person who can't make the meeting due to a schedule conflict.

Chapter 4
The List

Create a list of 5-12 people you would like to invite to your club. If you're not sure where to begin, think about the co-worker who you always see reading a book during lunch break, your cousin who loves Zane's books or your friend who loves Dan Brown's novels and then write their names down.

Once you jot down one name, you will begin to think of other people you would like to invite to your club. But don't over think this process. If you can only think of 3 people that's ok, you don't need to have a club with starting membership of 25 people for it to be successful. Small gatherings actually work great for first time meetings since your first meeting will be mostly you and the members coming up with a book club name, bylaws and ideas you have for your club and future meetings.

Also, use this chance to reach out to people you always wanted to get to know better but for whatever reason never had the opportunity. Now is a great time to connect with others and make new friends. If you plan to have open membership, consider printing flyers; include your meeting information (date, time, location and book selection) and posting them at book stores, libraries, coffee shops and your local colleges.

Chapter 5
Taking it Public

Once you create a list of people you would like to invite to the club send them an invite. You can use www.evite.com, www.mypunchbowl.com or simply send an email or text message. For a nice touch, write out invites and mail it to your potential members. If you would like to mail out pre-printed invitations instead, check out www.vistaprint.com. They have a wide variety of invitations that may interest you for free. On your invitation ask everyone to bring along a booklover friend as this will be a great way to meet other literary divas and grow your membership list at the same time.

Invites should include:

1. Name of club (if you already selected it)
2. Date, Time, and Location of Meeting
3. Hostess Name
4. BOTM
5. Food items suggestions for your guest to bring (if you're not buying are making all the food items yourself)
6. Request they bring a friend, BOTM, pen, and notepad

Chapter 6
Nuts and Bolts

If you decide to wait for your first meeting to name your club, be sure to make this item the first thing on your agenda. Collectively come up with a name that reflects your purpose and interest of the group itself. I named my book club, *Nubian Sistas Book Club* to reflect our unity and sisterhood. "Nubian" was selected to honor the African tribe filled with beautiful and intelligent women and also as a way to reflect our club's goal to focus only on AA books. "Sistas" represented our close knit group of family members and friends who are more like sisters to one another.

Other great book club names I love are: *Sister Circle Book Club, Ladies Literary Society, Reading Between the Lines, Club Mimosa, APOOO (A Place of Our Own)* and *Divine Divas Book Club*.

During the meeting, create a list of bylaws for your club. According to dictionary.com, "bylaws are the law(s) or rules governing the internal affairs of an organization (dictionary.com)." Keep the bylaws short, to the point and easy to follow.

For example, a bylaw could be "If you miss more than three meetings in a row, your membership may be terminated" or "Respect your fellow divas during the book discussion." Create bylaws or rules that will help your club run more smoothly and will settle any issues or disputes that may come up in the future. Think about the book club's purpose when creating your bylaws and I suggest you have a general idea of a couple of rules you would like to implement beforehand. Then talk to your members about your ideas during the meeting and create the list together.

While creating bylaws, you may or may not want to include consequences. But please remember, if you create too many strict rules, you will lose your members before your club even gets off the ground. Keep it simple, keep it respectful, and remember the point of your club is to enjoy each other company while discussing books not to create a new communist country.

Create a process for selecting officers or assigning duties. Some officer titles you can use are: President, Vice President, Secretary and Treasurer. You can also use titles like: Event Coordinator, Head Diva and Book and Food Committee. Create jobs and titles that will best fit your club needs.

Chapter 7
The Meeting

So you did it. You invited your BFFs over for an evening of titillating book discussions and you have your home ready for their arrival. Now the fun part begins. You're ready to host your first meeting.

Book club meetings usually last about 2 hours and include food items from full course meals to appetizers, drinks, and deserts. You could ask everyone to bring a small dish and turn it into a pot luck lunch or have a simple brunch. The choice is yours.

During your first meeting, you will discuss the BOTM as well as discuss future meeting dates, the next hostess, your next BOTM selection and the general direction of your book club. This is the perfect time to get everyone's feedback on how to make your book club the best club possible. As your club continues to grow, begin having conversations about possibly doing volunteer work in the community or taking your club online and reaching as many readers as possible. Discuss attending different literary events in your community and make plans to take a trip together. Don't limit your club to just the living room. Begin exploring the many facets of the literary world around you. From book fairs to book cruises, you'll be surprised what is available to book clubs and book lovers now-a-days.

Conclusion

Enjoying the company of your fellow literary divas while discussing books and eating great food will soon become one of the highlights of your month. By sharing my fool-proof plan with you, it is my hope that this e-book will help you organize your book club quickly and effectively.

For more information on hosting a book club meeting, please read my book, *A Literary Divas Guide to Hosting a Fab Book Club Meeting*. It includes games, a list of ongoing literary events, meeting agenda template, BOTM selections, reading guides, literary diva tips and insights from other book club members across the country. The book is available for purchase online at www.thebookclubexpert.com and as a special bonus; all book purchases include a free membership to the Lit Diva Network.

Also, if you have any questions, comments or would like to share your book club information, ideas and/or stories, please contact me at nubianlit@gmail.com. You never know, I may feature your book club in the next edition of *A Literary Divas Guide to Hosting a Fab Book Club Meeting*!

If you enjoyed reading this book, please leave a review at www.barnesandnoble.com. It will be greatly appreciated.

This Page Intentionally Left Blank

Made in the USA
Columbia, SC
27 April 2017